The Kitchen Mystic

To Roseann —

Thanks for your writing
inspiration in the
Phoenix —
Warmly,
Mary

To my husband Fred,
one of my teachers.

—MARY HAYES GRIECO

Hazelden Educational Materials
Center City, Minnesota 55012-0176

ISBN: 0-89486-814-4

Editor's note
Hazelden Educational Materials offers a variety of information
on chemical dependency and related areas. Our publications do not
necessarily represent Hazelden's programs, nor do they officially
speak for any Twelve Step organization.

The Kitchen Mystic

*Spiritual Lessons
Hidden in Everyday Life*

Mary Hayes-Grieco

HAZELDEN

Contents

Foreword

Many of us who join Twelve Step recovery programs do so out of crisis—the pain of our own addiction or perhaps the addiction of someone else brought us there. Recovery has come to mean something unique and individual to each one of us, but to most of us it has come to mean traveling on a spiritual path toward a healthy unity of mind, body, and spirit, a clear look at personal assets and liabilities, and a sense of community through shared experience, strength, and hope.

A Twelve Step program can give us a framework for infinite personal growth and spiritual awareness when we realize that it is not rigid dogma, strictly applied, but rather a doorway to a personal spirituality, rooted in the heart of the principles and traditions.

In the beginning, new to recovery, we are still trying to regain our equilibrium and balance, and we may be mostly focused on our addictions and immediate problems. But later, when life looks like it might be worth living after all, we have the incentive and support to work on some of our unhealthy patterns, healing wounds that may go back to childhood.

Eventually, we discover that we are infinitely more than *this addiction* or *that problem*. Our new sense of values and self-esteem motivate us to become a part of a larger world. There is a silent evolution going on within us, an emerging spirit that guides us to learn more about our connection to other human beings and all of life, and to express our spiritual nature in day-to-day living.

As we spiritually awaken, we develop a new outlook, a new perspective on what the possibilities are. Some of us have a strong spiritual curiosity and become spiritual explorers, looking to many sources for insights we can apply to our lives. Many of us become interested in pursuits we never before saw as relevant. For some, it becomes useful to learn about other great spiritual traditions, both Eastern and Western, because we discover that common wisdom and themes we can resonate with were there all along. We may learn the teachings of spiritual leaders like Lao Tsu, Christ, Buddha, or Native American elders, adopting ageless wisdom that speaks directly to us.

Millions of people now find themselves on a spiritual pathway. For a great many of us, our recovery from addiction or other serious life problems provided the entry point, the doorway to a life that became far more than absence of misery.

And our journeys are highly individual because we are all different.

Mary Hayes-Grieco is a spiritual explorer. Mary's writing gives clarity about what we can do when we look beyond our problems and see that we are much more. Indeed, inherent in each one of us is an individual expression in a world that we no longer identify as revolving around us. Our definition of ourselves has outgrown the labels and limitations of our early days of recovery. Mary writes about her own experiences and what works for her, but her colorful essays may give you insights to use as your own spiritual path unfolds. I hope you enjoy her vitality, humor, and wisdom, and that they light the spark of a mystic in you.

Judith Delaney
Editor
Summer 1992

The Kitchen Mystic

I'd like to suggest a new name for the spirituality that is spreading like a quiet fire through our society. I see it in myself and seekers around me who have passed through and incorporated the gifts of different paths. It's a kind of synthesis of Judeo-Christian principles, yoga, Twelve Step philosophy, Earth religions, and New Age paradigms: I call it Kitchen Mysticism.

Mysticism is defined as "the belief in the direct, intimate union of the soul with God, through contemplation and love." The kitchen is where you perform important mundane acts such as cooking, eating, washing dishes, and telling the truth with your close friends. Kitchen Mysticism is a path that cultivates the awareness of direct, intimate union with the Divine in the arena of

everyday mundane existence. It's a very personal path, and there are as many ways of walking it as there are people.

Kitchen Mystics may or may not attend an organized church. They find so many convenient places to commune and worship: the shower, the car, a park bench at sunset. You will often spot the Mystics muttering earnestly aloud to Someone no one else can see, or stopping mid-project with an entranced look . . . listening. They are performing one of the major practices of the faith: conducting an ongoing, loving dialogue between the God Within and the God Without.

Kitchen Mystics have rich internal lives and so have smaller appetites for external stimulation than other people. We pay for entertainment less often because we see that truth is stranger than fiction anyway. We passionate spiritual seekers find ourselves involved in a never-ending mystery story that is unfolding with subtlety, finesse, and occasional high drama. There is a benevolent plot afoot, and the conspirators are everywhere—seen and unseen. Their mission: the total destruction of our fears and limitations, resulting in our final spiritual awakening! It's harrowing, it's uplifting, and it's more thrilling than "Star Trek" because we ourselves are the main characters! We Kitchen Mystics keep each other vastly entertained with accounts of the latest synchronicity and break-through insights we are experiencing.

Mystics find meaning in many places. God is always hiding clues and love letters for us in the people and scenery of daily life, and it's fun to dis-cover these. It's like an Easter egg hunt: I wink and nod at my Friend when I have found another colored egg, and we laugh together at the humor and cleverness with which it was hidden in plain sight. If I am struggling to uncover a new under-standing, I hear a voice whispering to me: "Warm . . . warmer . . . cooler . . . warmer . . . HOT!" I will eventually find it or be taken gently by the hand and have it shown to me before I feel too dejected.

Almost every Kitchen Mystic has a special object of contemplation and worship, something from the physical world that says "God" directly to you—and maybe no one else! My daughter sees the Divine in a common rock. When she was tiny and I was trying to hustle her into the car to go to daycare, she would stop several times as we crossed the street to pick up stones and talk to them. Then she'd put them in her pockets. Now when we return from traveling, her suitcase is rattling with the inevitable stones that have called out to her as new friends. She won't let me dispose of them—they're sacred. White ones are extra-special, and she can spot a chip of white quartz in a bag of common fish-tank gravel and insist that I meditate on it with her. Personally, I don't "get" God in rocks, but I think it is important for Mystics to support each other's contemplations.

I see God in onions. I always have. I remember when I first saw my mother slicing into an onion when I was about six. I stopped my playing, awestruck. What is this vegetable that is so pure, so watery-white, so many-layered in concentric rings that make mounds of perfect circles as they fall open onto the cutting board? I begged her to let me cut some, despite her warning that it would make my eyes burn. I can remember the concentration and reverence welling up within me as I awkwardly tried to make perfect slices. My eyes *did* burn and I had to stop after a few cuts, but I vowed that I would understand onions some day and cook with them myself.

4

My contemplation of the Mystery in the onion continues to this day. As an artist I have paid homage to my friend the onion by creating a stained glass window of an underground bulb that now hangs in a local food co-op. As a cook I have learned how to coax the sweetness out of an onion, and to tame its fire into mellow good humor. I can cut them now without crying, but not without pausing for a brief moment. Red onions are especially divine. I hold a slice up to the sunlight pouring in through the kitchen window, and it glows like a fine piece of antique glass. Cool watery-white with layers delicately edged with imperial purple . . . strong, humble, peaceful . . . with that fiery nub of spring green in the center, aspiring to sprout and become more . . . "Ah! Look at *this* one!" I cry to my husband and daughter nearby. They look at each other and smile at me tolerantly. "That's a really nice one." They don't "get" God in onions the way I do, but they know that we Mystics have to stick together.

> *Sultan, saint, pickpocket—love has everyone*
> *by the ear, drawing us to God by secret ways.*
> *I never knew that God, too, desires us.*
>
> —*Rumi*

Spirituality and Religion

"Don't throw the baby out with the bath water," the old saying goes. This is a valuable saw when it comes to spirituality and religion. In recent years I have heard former churchgoers say, "I'm a recovering Catholic," as if referring to a dangerous disease. And I have heard church leaders giving their congregations dire warnings about the "New Age" spirituality. They criticize it for being scattered and shallow, or worse, the direct conspiracy of the devil. I feel frustrated and sad when I hear this polarization between tradition and a personal, open-ended spiritual search, because there is a need for both of these things. In my life, it's time to bring spirituality and religion together.

What's the distinction between spirituality and religion? Many people don't believe there is one.

Yet all of us have known kind, gentle souls who never entered a church in their lives, as well as detestable people who went to church every Sunday. Religions, in and of themselves, don't necessarily produce spiritual people. And people can grow and have spiritual lives whether they go to church or not.

My definition of spirituality is, *The cultivated awareness that I am an individual expression of an immortal Self whose nature is love, peace, and creativity.* Let's take this apart to understand it better. *Awareness* means being cognizant, conscious, and knowing in a responsive way. It is a state of being and perception rather than a collection of beliefs. You develop it with education and training, helpful techniques, and ongoing attention. *Cultivated awareness* is that state of awareness you deliberately grow, like a gardener.

An individual expression of an immortal Self means that I am a small but important part of something much greater than I. There is something that was here before I became who I am now, and it will exist after I lay this body-personality down at my death. I am that something, that Self, temporarily expressing myself here in this time. This Self is also expressing itself all around me as the different people, creatures, and objects that make up what we call the world. Like water in the ocean we are defined as drops for a short time, but we are always part of the whole ocean that exists before, during, and after we express ourselves individually in the material world. The nature of the Self is *love, peace,* and *creativity.* The Self has many other qualities too. These are the spiritual qualities that religions have attempted to instill in us for ages: faith, hope, joy, compassion, courage, kindness, universal brotherhood, strength.

The challenge of our spiritual journey is to heal and clarify our individual personalities on all levels—physical, emotional, intellectual, and spiritual—so that we can experience these spiritual qualities, not just hope for and think about them. We think that we are human beings seeking a divine experience, but the key to our spiritual liberation is realizing that we are divine Beings having a human experience. We are Spirit, enjoying a risky sojourn as a higher mammal on planet Earth.

Our bodies and psyches are thick and dark with pain and ignorance, like a lamp with a blackened glass chimney. "We see as through a glass, darkly." The spiritual journey is the cleaning and polishing of the glass so that the burning light within may radiate outward, illuminating itself and its environment. As we become enlightened, we embody more and more energy and happiness in our direct knowledge that we are an expression of God. Anything we do in our daily lives to cultivate more of this love, peace, and creativity is a spiritual practice. Spirituality is a personal matter, and every one of us has a completely unique spiritual journey.

Many people today are exploring spirituality with great independence and zeal. We flit from flower to flower like enthusiastic hummingbirds—a little yoga here, a little shamanism there, a chapter or two of inner-child work, six of the Twelve Steps. There's always something beckoning us to new levels of love, freedom, and power. Today, spiritual seekers have broken from distorted, shame-based religion and are reveling in a buffet of other religions as well as in the new ideas of expanding consciousness.

For me, that was fine and good for a number of years. It was exactly what I needed to do. But after a while, I was dissatisfied with traveling a little way on many different paths, and I began to think that perhaps religious monogamy wasn't such a bad idea. As in many relationships, an open-ended situation can take you only so far. There is something extremely valuable for me now in committing to the parameters of a whole religion. It is the challenge and the gift of a deepening experience—diving below the sparkling surface and meeting the fears, the problems, the dark side, the Mystery. I know in my heart that my spiritual journey will take me to new edges, new frontiers, and beyond them to real fulfillment if I have the courage and discipline to stay on this special path. I am ready to bring my spirituality and my religion together and settle down.

A religion can be our path of spiritual exploration. It can provide us with community, rituals, rules, limits, mythology, inspired writings, spiritual practices, and models of spiritual mastery. Every true religion has a wellspring of transforming spiritual energy. A living religion is whole and internally consistent. There is an overall balance and integrity to this path that brings depth and richness to seekers as they mature.

Many people take part in religion's rituals because they are part of what is expected socially. Some people are ready to do more spiritual work, while others observe from a safe comfort zone. There's nothing wrong with the latter. Onlookers can glean spiritual benefits from observing a religious community. Everyone proceeds at his or her own pace.

Oftentimes the most enthusiastic participants in a church are converts. They don't have the built-in resentments toward the religion of their youth. As a result, something of the fresh living Spirit reaches out and taps them, smiling. *Come,* it says. This is true for my cousin Betsy. She married a Muslim and became a follower of Islam. She wholeheartedly embraced it, to the dismay of all her Catholic relatives and feminist friends. They shuddered with horror at her new practices— keeping her head veiled, disappearing for prayers three times a day, accepting her defined role as wife and mother. Her social circle dwindled to practically nothing, then eventually began to expand into the Muslim community, where this lifestyle was understood and accepted. I was intrigued and went to visit her.

Betsy and I spent a good part of the day together in her small, sunny apartment with our children. We talked about religion and our spiritual experiences. We wiped noses and made peanut butter snacks (apparently a universal concept) for the children. At precisely noon and precisely three, she disappeared for a few minutes of devotional prayer in the direction of Mecca. She moved in her small world with quiet grace and serene eyes, and demonstrated endless patience with her sticky, boisterous toddlers. She was happy. It was one of the most peaceful afternoons I had spent in a while, and as I took my leave my heart was full and rosy. I had been spiritually fed all day by a palpable glow of love and light that was established in the circle of their home. That day I enjoyed the mundane tasks of motherhood in a way my feminist beliefs had never allowed me to.

Many people these days are turning to Earth religions for their religious expression. Ordinary Lutheran folks are attending Native American pipe ceremonies, dancing a spiral dance at a Wiccan solstice, or seeking power animals to the beat of drums in a shamanistic journey. There is an important recognition going on: it is necessary to come once again into sacred relationship with our Mother Earth. People are turning toward religions where God is seen and celebrated as *immanent,* here inside of us and the land, not *transcendent,* in a faraway place called heaven.

This awareness is necessary for balance, but Native American leaders caution us. They don't want us to be casual about their religion, to be without real awareness and respect for it. Native elders often say to Christians, "Turn to your own roots. There is power there. There is Spirit. Go to the roots of your own religion and make it belong to you."

I took this advice and looked to my own tradition. I had maintained a connection to it in my heart, despite the fact that I hadn't been to church in years. I gave church a try, but I gave it up again when I got a tight, contracted feeling in my stomach and chest. I trusted my body's wisdom and decided to worship somewhere else.

I'm still too eclectic to make the kind of religious commitment that Betsy chose. I've settled into a synthesis of my religious roots and my other spiritual explorations. It's big enough for breathing room and small enough for focus and consistency. It's a braid of religious practice and understanding. I feel good about this braid in my life. Each strand contributes to the power and effectiveness of the others. And they all lead me into the same circle of wholeness.

Recently I went on a lovely retreat to a small Franciscan center run by two Catholic nuns. As I sat in their cozy living room by the fire, my eyes and my heart found rest in the pictures of Jesus and Mary that hung on the walls. The sun shone like fiery jewels through a round stained glass window that depicted a female form holding up the moon. As one of the sisters moved quietly through the room, I caught the wholesome scent of almond fragrance in sesame oil—she had just given a therapeutic massage. I did not hear the click of swinging rosary beads as I used to in school, but I was reminded still of those nuns of my childhood. As I sat there, I thought of them with love, as women with ideals, women with personal discipline, women living in community. I remembered how hard they had worked to instill the strength of religion in my soul. I realized with amazement that they had succeeded. I watched this modern sister go to the bookcase and pick up her Motherpeace tarot cards. She was going to her room to meditate near her statue of St. Francis. I watched the fire in the silent, sunlit room and realized I was home.

> *Kabir says: Listen, friend!*
> *My beloved Master lives inside.*
> —*Kabir*

Your Spiritual Teacher

*O*ne of the basic tenets of the spiritual seeker is, My life is a classroom. I am learning an important lesson from this experience. And there is a persistent hunger in many seekers to find a good spiritual teacher. I have learned that the Teacher is always here, now.

When I look behind me at my journey, I see an unbroken daisy chain of people and events that have brought me to where I stand. If I open my eyes to my circumstances today, I may recognize the class I am currently enrolled in and may feel the gentle, encouraging smile of the Teacher. The Teacher is always within me, my true Self, providing circumstances and instructors to grow me into my own wisdom.

The amount of joy or suffering we experience in daily life is in direct proportion to the grace with which we accept our role as students. We need to recognize the course we are enrolled in, if we can, and apply ourselves to the work at hand with zest and humility. And we need to give honor and thanks to the Teacher. Who is our Teacher? Exactly the people and situations that we are engaged with here, now.

Relationships are teachers. My twelve-year marriage feels like a tough graduate course: Trust, Vulnerability, and Mutual Respect 300. My daughter is teaching a course: Life is Fun 101. My best friend cheerfully nudges me past the limited gates of my own thinking, and rude neighbors help me ground the principles of unconditional love and forgiveness in my life.

You can learn a lot about yourself from people who elicit a strong response from you, positive or negative. These people are mirrors for your greatness or your flaws. Study your heroes. What seedling quality in yourself is in full flower in these people? Our heroes magnetize us to them to call forth our own embryonic excellence.

All of us have someone in our environment who is irritating, someone we just love to hate. This is a Teacher. There used to be a woman in my life who was very annoying, and she wouldn't go away. I bumped into her *everywhere*. After several years, I realized that this woman demonstrated the same insecurities I possessed, the ones that I had quietly hidden from myself and others. I practiced compassion and acceptance toward her as a step in greater love for myself. I don't ever see her anymore—I guess I don't need to.

Even an outright enemy is valuable. People who attack us provide us with a golden opportunity to develop more confidence, self-esteem, and boundaries. Sometimes we don't tackle these lessons unless we really need to. This is where the practice of expressing gratitude comes in. Gratitude is one of the fastest tracks to the peace and strength of the Higher Self. If we can say, "Thank you for this opportunity to become more my Self"—and try to mean it—we make quick progress in the classrooms taught by our adversaries.

Some people actually carry the title of "teacher." In this case, they may be real spiritual teachers or maybe helpful technicians. A technician is someone who has a tool or technique that you can learn quickly and apply to your life to some benefit, but the actual person soon fades into the background of your life. There are a lot of technicians around these days.

Spiritual teachers—people who have truly become what they teach—are more rare. They walk their talk. It radiates from their pores. You find yourself wanting just to be with them, to watch them, to hang around "after class." There is something there that you need to imprint on yourself, as a baby goose does with its mother before it can fly. You carry these teachers in your heart all the days of your life.

I feel this way about one of my spiritual teachers. She writes and teaches about unconditional love, and in her presence, I see unconditional love in action. It is so beautiful to watch that I feel like following her around from room to room. She models for me the serenity and abundant energy of someone who has no inner conflicts. She serves the good of the whole effortlessly, like a clear spring of water continuously bubbling forth. The fact that she is eighty-two instead of thirty-seven probably helps, but I think her luminous clarity is the result of her diligence as a student to the teachers in her life.

The classrooms we learn the most in are the difficult situations apparently not of our choosing—situations in which we have little external control. The urge to fret and complain and resist is great, but we can attempt to collect ourselves and ask an important question: What spiritual principle is being called for here? Patience? Tolerance? Faith? Truth? Courage? Kindness? The sooner we get clear on the assignment and surrender to it with willingness and zest, the sooner we feel happy about the whole thing. And then something beautiful emerges within us.

On the other hand, some learning takes a long time to unfold, and it is necessary to thrash along by trial and error for a while. Sometimes we're in the dark without matches. We can drive ourselves mad asking, *What lesson is this? What am I supposed to be learning?* Don't worry—you're learning. You're just in the process, and you'll know when you know—and not before. Just keep doing what is right in front of you with as much love and focus as you can muster, and you can't go too far wrong!

Sometimes we just need to be in one place and allow ourselves to be slowly and steadily opened by the hundreds of duties and challenges that our responsibilities place before us each day. Think of this process as the opening of a peony in June. It sits there on its long stalk with the life-force swelling upward into a hard round bud. And then along come the ants! Hundreds of tiny ants stream up the stem and swarm all over the bud, gently pestering the flower to uncurl her petals and let them in to experience her nectar. For over a week the ants make their way slowly inside the petals, layer after layer. They just keep tromping around, assisting the flower to open herself fully to the sunlight. They are serving the life-force. And then one day you look and there is this absolutely gorgeous flower breathing fragrance and color into space with unabashed extravagance. If you cut this perfect specimen and put it in a crystal vase on your table, you will still encounter quite a few dedicated ants! And like these ants in the peony,

there are some lessons in our lives that will probably come in installments until the day we die—
trust, vulnerability, intimacy. . . .

There are, however, a few courses that I know I
have actually completed, and I have felt the smile
of my teachers as they put a star on my chart. At
these rare and precious times, I feel a sense of
wholeness, and I understand the freedom in the
Native American declaration, "It is a good day
to die!"

No man can reveal to you
ought but that which already lies half
asleep in the dawning of your own knowledge.
—Kahlil Gibran

23

Making Friends with Discipline

Serenity is a matter of personal discipline. Serenity is a stance that we choose, and we must build and reinforce it on a daily basis whether we are in the mood to do it or not.

Many people are allergic to the term *discipline,* perhaps because it is falsely associated with another word—*punishment.* This is understandable, since many of us were abused as children in the name of discipline. But in truth, the practice of personal discipline is an act of self-love. It is the way we turn our backs on a long, bleak history of abandonment and come home to ourselves. Making friends with discipline is one of the best things we can do for ourselves.

What is discipline? *Discipline is a set of attitudes and behaviors that I choose and practice with persistence to produce long-term health and happiness— whether or not I feel happy about doing it in the short term.* A recovering alcoholic employs discipline to get to an AA meeting, even though she doesn't feel like it. A parent who was abused as a child halts his knee-jerk response to hit his rebellious child, even though he feels as if he wants to. We may need to turn to self-discipline because our lives have become unmanageable, but discipline can become our lifelong ally and companion if we are serious about our spiritual journey.

Spiritual mastery will come to us as a result of becoming disciplined on all levels of the personality—physical, emotional, and mental. On the physical level, this means establishing good health habits, being financially responsible, keeping beauty and order in our environment, and walking in balance with the natural world. On the emotional level, it means handling feelings appropriately. We need to know how and when to feel, express, and release emotions, as well as when to detach from excessive sensitivity and emotionality. On the mental level, it is our responsibility to uproot negative conditioned beliefs in our minds and cultivate a positive, self-chosen worldview.

Ultimately, we are meant to be the masters of our minds and not the servants—to focus our thoughts or be silent at will. This is the goal of the discipline of meditation. As we make progress with disciplines on different levels, our personalities become clean and luminous for the inner Spirit to shine through. We can operate with more and more love and power for the well-being of everyone. This is a long-term project, but I can't think of a better way to spend life.

It is usually obvious what area of life is calling for self-discipline. We feel out of control, frustrated, and ashamed. Or maybe we are denying the problem, but we are getting consistent feedback from others that our lack of self-control is problematic for *them*. We are then asked to make a change that feels unnatural to us. In his book *The Road Less Traveled*, M. Scott Peck describes discipline as an "unnatural" act. It is certainly a radical act of the spiritual will. We make a commitment to an upward trend in our lives and choose new attitudes or behaviors.

At first it feels like pushing a boulder uphill. Progress is infinitesimal or erratic for a while, but this is deceptive—a lot of growth is going on underground. It is better to make some small, real changes than to make a big, heroic, noisy effort for several days and then completely forget about our commitment and backslide. That adds to our original hopelessness about our ability to change.

Practicing a new discipline without being attached to immediate results works best. We will make incremental progress and leave crisis behind. If we persist in the effort, we will begin to stabilize and gain glimpses of our mastery of this part of our lives. It is common at this point to want the "reward" of relaxing our discipline—and then comes the backslide! The painful fact remains that we must follow persistence with *more* persistence *and* vigilance. The old patterns of behavior have long, tough roots into our being, and many years of dominance. But if we continue to do what is good for us whether we feel like it or not, we build an utterly new foundation for the rest of our lives. There is a power in repetition that eventually realigns the patterns in our unconscious and allows us to become different creatures than we used to be.

Currently, my discipline is aimed at keeping my desk clean and organized. I grew up in alcoholic chaos, and this is a real dragon for me. The sight of a pile of papers to file elicits feelings of hopelessness and being overwhelmed! But the beat goes on—my past successes assure me that I can indeed become more organized despite my old emotions. A few years from now it will seem natural to have an orderly desk—another star on my chart.

Ten Steps to Discipline

Acknowledge the need to become more disciplined in how you live your life. Crack through any denial operating about your out-of-control behavior. Make the distinction between discipline and punishment—discipline is an act of love. Deal with the emotions of rebelliousness.

Seek inspiration. Most of the world's great leaders and performers have had tremendous personal discipline. Who are your heroes? Hang up their pictures. Let their excellence call you forward to realize your own aims.

Decide to become disciplined. Choose an area where there is a crying need. State your will to make a change with the help of your Higher Self. Say it aloud as a statement of your spiritual will: "I will become clean and organized." "I will become honest with myself and others." "I will finish what I start." "I will take the time to cook a good meal."

Enlist support. Choose friends who demonstrate personal discipline and learn from them. Tell your current friends and family that you are making some difficult changes and that you want their quiet, nonjudgmental support for your effort. Talk to your Higher Self about it often.

Release feelings of hopelessness. Hopelessness *will* come up when you try to change long-standing patterns. Feel it, cry or rage about it, but don't *believe* it anymore. Keep moving.

Stay on track. Remind yourself every morning what your discipline is and that it isn't optional. Do it. Post a copy of your will statement where you can see it. At night, review the day. Did you do what you needed to do today to produce long-term happiness? Check in with a friend about it at least once a week.

Acknowledge your progress. Celebrate glimpses of health and accomplishment in your chosen area of discipline.

Persist, persist, persist. Acquire a taste for repetition and good habits.

Stabilize in your new mode. Give yourself time to get used to new behaviors. Remember that they're still new. It can take years to stabilize, but it's worth it in the long term.

Be vigilant! Notice if you're relaxing your practices, and notice what happens to you and your life when you do. Remember the power of repetition. Try not to be compulsive or rigid, but remember that too much relaxation isn't a treat for you—it is self-abandonment.

> *What is the greatest obstacle*
> *to spiritual growth?*
> *Laziness . . .*
>
> —*Shankaracharya*

Planetary Recovery

*I*t seems as though most people I meet these days are familiar with the Twelve Steps because they or someone they know is in recovery from something. There are groups for recovering alcoholics, overeaters, gamblers, incest survivors, abusive parents, codependency, sex and love addiction, compulsive spending, and people who are powerless over their emotions. I'm sure the list is growing and new groups are germinating. "I'm from a dysfunctional family," people say. I have heard this statement so often in the past few years that I wonder if it's a new norm. I wonder if people will start forming support groups for folks who have had serene childhoods so they too can belong.

I can understand this. The recovery movement is one of the better opportunities to come along in

human society in quite a while. The Twelve Step program offers us what human beings want most: a chance to begin a spiritual journey with the support of compassionate community, a chance to come into a daily relationship with God on our own terms. It offers structure and support so we can leave desperation and isolation behind as we conduct a thorough self-inquiry and personal housecleaning. It offers daily practices to establish and deepen serenity, and the joyful duty of serving others who need our help from the full cup of our own experience. Ultimately, the gifts of a long-term, active participation in the program far outweigh the previous anguish.

In truth, we all come from a large dysfunctional family—the human race. As a whole, we are approaching the point of "hitting bottom" worldwide. Our life here on Planet Earth has become unmanageable. Our ecological problems at this point are so huge, and our society so out of control, that humanity is at the classic decision point: self-destruction or recovery? As in many dysfunctional families, some people are playing the chief role in acting out this destruction, while others live in victimization or denial. People in the recovery and spiritual growth movements are the vanguard of change in the system. Like the family member who begins recovery long before the alcoholic will admit the problem, we can only diligently work our program, speak our truth, witness the inevitable bottom as it comes, and hope for the best outcome.

The recovery and spiritual growth movements may be the evolutionary thrust that leads the human race out of the mess our mass ignorance and addictions have created. According to Brian Swimme, physicist and philosopher, nature improves on her designs throughout time with the experimentation of certain "fringe groups" in a species. A species is going along and maintaining a certain status quo, and somehow a little group becomes isolated from the rest of the others. This group becomes free to experiment and innovate with their food or social habits and eventually stumbles upon a way that is more efficient and pro-survival. They adopt these ways and teach them to their offspring. After a few generations, the new way is established, and the experiment becomes instinct. Mysteriously, the rest of the species also develops the new way. They "resonate" the greater strength that has begun in one strand of the community, and evolutionary change takes place.

The recovery movement certainly began as a "fringe group." The desperation and social isolation that chronic alcoholics had long known set the stage in the 1930s for the new experiment of AA. Those first AA groups built their strength and success in relative isolation from the rest of society. For a long time they were treated with suspicion and misunderstanding by the general public. But they had stumbled upon something that worked, something that was pro-survival. For the first time, alcoholics got better and began to function well in their lives. AA resolutely preserved the purity of the successful elements by adhering to strong principles. And the resonance grew. Sunny and simple, AA groups began to spread with the inevitability and persistence of the common dandelion. Now millions of people around the world gather and grow together in AA groups, and the word *recovery* is a common word in today's vocabulary.

I am intrigued with the fast proliferation of addiction-specific clones of the original Twelve

Step program. Why is it that there are so many people who are bottoming out on *something?* Why has life become unmanageable for so many people? Maybe the recovery movement is the prelude to something else. It is said that religion is "a finger pointing at the moon," but it is not the moon itself. I have a feeling that recovery too is a finger pointing at something, but it is not the end in itself. There is something else. There is something underneath our species-wide addiction problems that is calling out for evolutionary change.

What is humanity bottoming out on, fundamentally? What are we recovering *toward?* Some people say we are bottoming out on the destructive extremes of the patriarchal-warrior cult that began to overtake societies several thousand years ago. This is the hierarchical, male-dominated model that holds dominance, competition, and control as its chief values. In this model, resources are scarce, and we need to fight somebody to get them so *our* tribe will be okay. Somebody's always up and somebody's always down, and the world is rife with possible enemies to attack or defend ourselves from. Oppression and exclusion are just part of the game, and the players are always shifting positions.

Humans have steadily lost their connection with nature, with the wisdom of the body, feelings, and soul. "Developed" societies are filled with people who feel lonely and spiritually malnourished. We turn to addictive substances to silence the internal howling that is trying to get our attention and have us face the truth of our situation. If we're very lucky, we bottom out early and get into recovery.

In the last half of this century, certain groups in our developed societies have been experimenting with a new paradigm. Spiritual seekers are adventurers seeking out a new world. We are creating this world right now in our small circles of people. Every little recovery group in a chilly church basement is one more vibrating cell resonating change. Our groups are strong enough now that they have the interest and attention of popular culture.

Time has come full circle for us here on Planet Earth in the 1990s. We are looking for a "new world," but it is a world we have known here before. According to Riane Eisler in *The Chalice and the Blade*, new archaeological evidence shows us that societies lived here for thousands of years in peace and wholeness before the bloody times of our recorded history. It is good for us to collectively remember that we are not fundamentally war-like just by virtue of being human. We are merely at the dangerous extreme of a long-term exploration into the limits of control over ourselves and our natural world. We can grow beyond it and learn to live in relaxed loving presence with ourselves, each other, the Planet Earth, and our Creator.

The day will come when, after harnessing
the winds, the tides, the gravitation, we shall harness
for God the energies of love. And on that day,
for the second time in the history of the world,
man will have discovered fire.
—*Teillhard de Chardin*

The Serenity Prayer—
It's All There

God grant me the serenity
To accept the things I cannot change,
The courage to change the things I can,
And the wisdom to know the difference.

I am beginning to see why the Serenity Prayer is an indispensable part of every Twelve Step gathering. It contains the sum total of what spiritual life is: a series of lessons about when to accept life as it is, and when to make changes for the better. You can say this prayer thousands of times and find it meaningful, because at any given time we need to employ acceptance, courage, or wisdom to feel

peace of mind in the moment. For many years of recovery we must employ these concepts, but eventually, we become them in our beings.

In a way, this prayer is a global contemplation: the wisdom of the East and West meets here. The wisdom of the East teaches us to accept life, for there is nowhere you have to go; it's all right here. Everything you see is equally One: God's consciousness in a myriad of forms. Be at peace with what you are, here, now. Accept. The wisdom of the West says, "You can be something more than you are right now—strive for it! Life can be better; you can use your knowledge and will to make changes that advance evolution. There is no problem that cannot be solved, and no creative innovation beyond your reach if you desire it. Courage!"

It is the wisdom of the Whole that knows which wisdom must predominate *now,* though each is bound to the other, inseparable partners in the dance of creation through time.

The truth in the Serenity Prayer must be horse sense because my little daughter understands it. She gave me a fine lesson about it one night. I was in a stew about something and she said, "Is there anything you can do about that?" I thought about it and replied that I couldn't. "Well then, Mom, I guess you'll just have to enjoy your own life," she told me matter-of-factly.

How did she figure that out at such a young age? There were adult children by the thousands all over the nation at that very moment struggling to fix everything wrong in their lives or feeling unable to make any changes in their lives. I guess she never "unlearned" her basic human wisdom.

Those of us who grew up in dysfunctional homes *need* the basic human wisdom of the Serenity Prayer. We are out of balance most of the time because we are not truly accepting life as it is, or we are not confidently using our wills to make the changes we need to in order to make our lives better. We live trying lives.

Several years ago my Inner Self told me, "You must give up *trying.*" *Trying what?* I wondered. Before long I began to realize that "trying" had been my baseline approach to life and that it was extremely stressful. I had been *trying* for so long—

trying to win my dad's admiration, trying to save my family of origin from alcoholic collapse, trying to be liked.

Trying is the opposite of peace and success. We have to really accept life as it is *and* use our skillful spiritual wills to open our lives to their fullest potential. Period. No more trying. It is the *commitment* to living this paradox fully that brings both serenity and excellence to a human life.

How do you gain acceptance of life as it is? My guess is that a healthy person in a healthy society would gain this acceptance in the normal process of gaining maturity. You get to know and accept yourself, train your abilities, and then use them in service to others. Accept your duties, accept others, accept the miracle of new life and the mystery of death. Accept the challenges of your generation and its contribution to society. Acceptance grows in an incremental way, like the ring of new wood that the tree gains each year.

It's harder when you have to dig yourself out of crippling childhood pain. But the years bring maturity and acceptance anyway, if we are open to it. Life itself teaches acceptance of life. Eventually we learn certain lessons: Nobody's perfect, especially me. I can't permanently keep anybody—people change, die, move away. When a relationship is over, no matter how much love there was, it's over. I can't keep any thing—things get lost, worn, outdated.

As we continue to mature, acceptance is no longer a thought or a process; it is a relaxed, open state of being. It is the state of being both empty and full simultaneously, established in the present, a container of positive potential in every moment, for everyone.

The free and powerful human beings—enlightened masters—live in this manner. These saints have become so established in the acceptance of life as it is that they are radiant lights of peace, love, and joy, regardless of their environment or circumstances. And yet the will of their personalities is so powerfully aligned with the Divine Will that miraculous things are accomplished through them all the time, with no effort. No trying! They choose to enhance the liberation of other people with calm detachment. They are able to see perfection in imperfection! This is the human potential contained in seedling form in the Serenity Prayer.

God grant me the serenity
To accept the things I cannot change,
The courage to change the things I can,
And the wisdom to know the difference.
—Serenity Prayer

Create Your Reality?

Some people say that it's the biggest turning point in human thought since the Copernican revolution. In the last decade or so, large numbers of people have embraced the idea that the reality each of us experiences is a projection of our own consciousness, and that we have some say about what that reality will be. We are not victims of anything, we hear. We can decide how we want things to be—and create it! The sky's the limit! As a spiritual counselor, I have welcomed this blithe notion with mixed emotions. On one hand, I agree. This is taking responsibility for your life and seeing the learning possibility in every situation. It's the end of a victim mind-set and the beginning of claiming our full spiritual power. On the other hand, I also know people who feel there shouldn't be any *limits* in their lives, and if there

are, then they must be doing something wrong. They're embarrassed because they think they should be creating a more attractive reality than they can show their friends at this moment. They *should* have more *control* over things than they do.

I've made it my personal job to say, "Yes, but . . ." about creating your reality, and I have investigated some of the fine print. I know we aren't supposed to say "can't" in these days of limitless possibility, but someone's got to do it. I now present my Mindful Maxims as a consumer warning if you subscribe to this otherwise fine paradigm.

Mindful Maxims Concerning Creating Your Reality

You can't create what you can't receive. If you don't truly feel *deserving* enough to have a kind mate or a new car, you won't get them until at least some of your toes are firmly planted on the new ground of being deserving. You have to work on your attitude first.

You can't create a new attitude by next week.
You can start today and persist through next week,
but you need to stick with it for much longer than
that before your attitude change reaches deep
enough to change your outer experiences.

***You can't create a new reality from your con-
scious mind if you still carry an old belief
buried in your unconscious.*** Sometimes you have
to be a detective to discern what negative belief
must be operating to create a repetitive unhappy
reality. It could be from a buried childhood event
or a past life. Hypnosis, dream work, or a session
with a reliable professional may help you dig it
out and look at it. Then you can change it.

***You can't go from nothing to everything
overnight.*** That usually takes years, even decades.
It is very unlikely that you will be lifted from

poverty with a lottery ticket or be asked to appear on a big-money game show. Upgrading your economic reality goes in steps and stages. You might have to go to school next, or you might have to plan some other practical strategy for raising your income. You will have to keep healing into greater self-esteem and personal power to be able to attract greater financial opportunities.

You can't move on to new situations until you have completely embraced and participated in the one you are in. The present is also your creation. What is here? Have you brought as much love and intelligence to your current situation as you can? Have you embraced the spiritual lesson inherent in this current opportunity? It's like school—you need to complete your current course work before you enroll in the next level of learning.

You can't create something that is incorrect for your personal spiritual journey. You already created this life, theoretically, to learn and accomplish certain things. You can't completely change the program halfway through.

You can do anything, but you can't do it without God's help.

God will help, but God won't do it for you.

Maybe you can have it all, but you can't have it all at the same time. Life is a game, some people say, but every game has rules and limits that define what the challenge is. On earth our challenge is a friendly struggle between desires and duties, time limits and limitless possibilities. That's why reincarnation makes practical sense in most religious systems. There are so many ways of playing this game that once isn't enough to exhaust our interest in it.

Limits give shape to your life. You came to earth because you desired to experience some things. You poured your limitlessness into a singular form that is known as you so that you could drink of life and be enjoyed by life. Maybe this is it. Be okay as you—limits and all.

Other than that, go for it!

> *If you have built castles in the air,*
> *your work need not be lost;*
> *that is where they should be.*
> *Now put the foundations under them.*
> *—Henry David Thoreau*

Giving and Receiving

*T*he ability to genuinely give and receive is such a conundrum for most recovering people. (A conundrum is a riddle or a complicated problem.) This is because we were grown in environments that were painfully out of balance in terms of healthy giving and receiving. Some people learned to give-give-give as a way of feeling valued and important. Others learned to take everything they could get—more than their share—in an attempt to fill a gaping hole inside. As adults, these people often get into relationships with each other and engage in a frustrating dance of immature love that ends in alienation, guilt, and blame. In fact, both types of people, the ones who give too much and the ones who take too much, bear the same wound: it is the wound of the needy child.

Very few people in our world get all of their childhood needs met. (We are all part of the largest dysfunctional family currently known— the human race!) Children need to be thoughtfully grown by a centered pair of grown-ups, along with the support of an extended family and a community. They need to be protected, nourished, appreciated, and guided into unfolding their potential. In most families, you're doing pretty well if you get a modicum of protection and "three hots and a cot"—some don't even get that.

If our needs are not met as children, we become perpetually needy inside. As adults we may adapt to these painful unmet needs by becoming reckless givers with an exaggerated sense of responsibility toward others and an inability to receive what we need, even if it is staring us right in the face. Or we may be selfish and self-absorbed, unable to respond to the needs of others without feeling resentful and taken advantage of. We may have both of these attitudes in different areas of our lives.

Being human means having needs and having to meet the needs of others. There is no way around it. No one who is still unable to give and receive comfortably and appropriately has recovered. It's like breathing. You can't just breathe out constantly without breathing in, or "receiving in," the air again—you'll die. Neither can you take in the air and withhold your carbon dioxide from the environment. You have to give that back. A healthy human is meant to be constantly giving and receiving in an easy, steady rhythm, exactly like breathing. Breathe in, breathe out. Breathe in, breathe out. Receive, give. Receive, give. Simple. For adult children of dysfunctional families, the simplicity of this basic function must be regained by steady self-healing. Fortunately, we can do this.

It is human nature to yearn toward wholeness. Even when you are choosing the wrong people and situations and replaying your original wounds, you are actually attempting to heal yourself. Subconsciously you choose people and situations that resemble your family. You think, *If only I try hard, I can fix this person and then he or she will meet my needs.* As you probably know, it never works that way. You cannot successfully fill a frozen need of the past by controlling someone in the present. You can never do it "right enough," and the person will tire of you and leave you with your gaping hole and a fresh wound to lick.

To heal the needy child within, you need to have your face turned continuously to the nourishing presence of the Higher Self. You can accept God as Mother and Father and entrust your needs, your vulnerability, and your innocence once again to a Parent who won't let you down. This Spirit is enormously talented at providing you with people and circumstances to steadily heal your wounds, meet your needs, and bring you into balance. It wants to help you move into greater harmony! You just need to be willing to receive what is coming to you and give what life is asking you to give.

Many people are afraid to receive. They feel guilty, afraid they are not deserving of something good, especially when they haven't asked for it. Or they fear they are depriving someone else by accepting something that they need. Some people are afraid to receive because they believe they will become vulnerable to another's manipulation or be "in debt" to the person giving. It takes a right understanding and good self-esteem to be able to receive the goodness life is capable of giving us.

This understanding and this self-esteem can be gained in steady increments as soon as you are willing to st-r-e-t-c-h open to it a bit at a time. A local teacher refers to this ability to receive and contain life's goodies as your "level of having-ness."

It takes a certain amount of trust and vulnerability to receive good things—you have to be willing to be open to the unexpected. You may need to acknowledge that someone else really sees you and your need and cares enough about you to serve that need *freely*. I have a neighbor who is a single mother of seven kids, all living at the poverty line. Every time she sees me she tells me how exhausted she is. And yet when I sincerely offer her some kind of help she refuses it. I finally realized that she is unwilling to be vulnerable to me and my caring. She wants to struggle along with what is familiar and complain about it because she doesn't want to open up her heart to unexpected human compassion. Why? Maybe because she'll cry. Sometimes you need to cry in order to receive. You need to feel and release old pain instead of running from it and remaining in a rut. People who are more interested in transformation than total control will walk forward into the unfamiliar realms of greater good, even as they tremble with fear and uncertainty.

The ability to genuinely give also requires a right understanding. You have probably experienced the sweet exhilaration and openness of true giving at times, but at other times when you gave you may have felt drained or resentful afterwards. Why the latter? You might have felt drained for one of three reasons:

You were giving with a motive and an attachment to a certain outcome or response from the other person. This is *not* giving, it is manipulation!

*You were giving to someone who was **taking**, but not able to **receive**.* Think about that one for a while.

You were giving beyond what was really practical for you to do. Our time, energy, and resources are valuable, and a certain amount of control is necessary.

One day you may be sitting in a cafe when an acquaintance sits down to tell you her problems. It is practical for you to lend a helping ear, and you choose to do that. Giving and receiving take place, and you both feel good about the encounter. If, however, your purpose in sitting there is to be alone with your own thoughts, and this person sits down and begins to talk, you cannot really give to her. You need to be true to your own intentions and inform her in an open-hearted way that you really don't want to talk to anyone right now. Your honesty is the best gift to both of you at that moment.

There are times when we are able to stretch our capacity for giving way beyond our previous practical limits. Certain special situations call forth from within us a wellspring of love and service, a perception that all giving is receiving, for there is only one Self that is both the servant and the recipient of that same love. This is the highest perception, and one that a serious spiritual seeker will eventually attain and become established in. Once Mother Teresa was asked, "How could you have personally picked up thousands of dying bodies from the streets of Calcutta?" She replied, "I have only lifted One."

The Creator gave us the Sun, our elder brother. It's his duty to give us warmth and to nourish the life-giving foods that are planted on Earth. And as we see, the Sun came up this morning, and shines on us, keeping us warm. He's doing his duty, and for this we are very grateful. So let us all put our minds together as one, and thank the Sun for still performing his duty. And let our minds be that way.
                                           —from a Thanksgiving speech
                                                      Onandagas elder

Everything's Not Under Control

"*Y*ou're so controlling!" I can't tell you how many times over the last ten years I have heard my husband exclaim this in a moment of exasperation. Adult children of alcoholics are notorious for controlling people and things in their environment.

My poor husband is often at the wrong end of my controlling behavior. I want to monitor how much he works, how much TV he watches, how he does his job as a father. He *should* be paying more attention to *me*. I also want to control my daughter—what she eats and what she wears. She *must* be healthy and socialized.

Doesn't reading that make you tense? I must be tense whenever I am controlling. It seems to me,

now, that the need to feel in control of everything is a by-product of an essential lack of trust in life. When I am controlling, I am trying to make everything all right because I *don't* know and *don't* trust that everything really *is* all right. Now I see that I need to go to a new level of faith and trust in my Higher Power. This means coming into a right relationship with "control."

The correct exercise of control is such a human dilemma. As a species, humans love control! We want to control our environment, our physical and emotional safety, our financial security, our self-image. We tend to want to control others or be controlled by them. We create roles, habits, rules, and personal and political systems out of the need to control. We're good at this, and a lot of it is necessary to establish a baseline of order and a healthy status quo. And yet it is this same passion for control that gets us into trouble—as individuals and as a species. If we do not exercise wisdom, control can easily become addiction, tyranny, and repression. Then we find ourselves rebelling against excessive control with a cry of "Freedom!" and we take refuge in creative chaos. Eventually the need for structure re-emerges if we are serious about manifesting our ideas in the world around us.

If you are serious about discovering and fulfilling your purpose, you must establish a right relationship with control on every level of your being: physical, emotional, mental, and spiritual. The point of having *some* control over your world is to have a foundation upon which to dance with life's spontaneity.

Life's creative unpredictability is both unsettling and delicious. We really have no ultimate control over most of it. But we can trust life anyway if we come into a correct relationship with control on an emotional level. There's really nothing you can't handle as long as you can have your feelings about it and be able to share them with others. People, jobs, and homes will come and go in your life, bringing up lots of feelings. Everyone has his or her own cache of buried pain waiting to erupt to the surface for healing. Our organism is always yearning toward health and wholeness, and our life situations will repeat the drama of our early wounds until we fully feel and heal them.

One of the common problems of addiction is the desire to control and repress the experience of painful emotions. If you spend your time and money on substances or projects designed to prevent you from feeling painful emotions, you will remain on a limited track with your life, and your mind and body will become more rigid and less adaptable as you age. But if you realize that your pain is a gift, and if you are determined to trust life, you will use your time and resources to feel your pain and heal from it instead of avoiding it with an addiction. There are, however, some people who need to exert more control over their feelings because they are awash in emotion. They need to learn to contain their feelings and to discipline themselves to bring focus to their bodies, minds, and spirits.

There is one power you always have, and no one can ever take it away from you: the power to take a point of view. This is the correct way to have control on a mental level. We cannot control life, but we *can* cancel our expectations and accept that in some inexplicable way, all is well—even when things are *not* going as we expect them to. This is an empowering point of view you can adopt in any circumstance, and it keeps you from slipping into the sloppy stance of being a victim.

I met a woman the other day who really understands this. She is so alive and excited about her journey and the mysterious, inevitable unfolding of God's plan for her life. Last year she lost her job of eighteen years very suddenly in a company reorganization. Instead of blaming her superiors as they laid her off, she could hardly keep from smiling and exulting in the wonderful surprise God must have in store for her to move her along so abruptly!

I have been thinking that the current climate of insecurity most people have about their job security is really a blessing in disguise. Now that previously stable companies are merging and disappearing and reincarnating all over the place, masses of people are being forced to abandon their belief in an external source of control and security. They are turning to inner resources of serenity amid a sea of change, and they are starting to listen to spiritual impulses for a new direction in their lives. Security is and always has been a very temporal thing, subject to change. Serenity amid the rise and fall of the ten thousand things in life that are beyond our control is a much more precious commodity—and we can always choose to have it.

This is *self-control*. The challenge for self-control on a spiritual level is being willing to let go of control and follow our spiritual impulses. This is different from the scattered, uninformed impulsiveness of an adult child who is afraid to think through consequences. It is different from compulsion, which is rigid, repetitive, and familiar. Our inner being is constantly communicating to us its desire and direction through spontaneous impulses.

These impulses come to us as a flash in our mind's eye, or as a little voice in our mind saying, *Why don't you . . . ?* Sometimes it is the unselfconscious reaching out of our hand to touch someone we hardly know with compassion. When we act upon divine impulse there is a sense of stepping across the gap of the unknown into a new realm. Like a mountain climber in the crystalline air of the present moment, we have a quiet mind and relaxed concentration. For a moment, we suspend judgment and concerns about outcome and follow this impulse with trust and detachment. It is this willingness to walk through the beckoning doorway of possibility that brings adventure to life and opens us to receive from God more than we can imagine creating ourselves. Yet it is the control we skillfully employ in our personality that will enable us to contain this goodness and continue strengthening the foundation to hold more.

> *Life is what happens while you're*
> *busy making plans.*
> —*John Lennon*

Living in Contentment

I've got a problem. What will I do? I have been on a journey of self-healing for many years because I observed that I was making wreckage of myself and was a trouble to people I wanted to be close to. I have made a lot of progress. I am no longer terribly inappropriate or irresponsible. I am now trustworthy to myself and others. I have even accomplished some goals and gained respect in my community. My problem is, this journey has brought me to the borders of an unfamiliar country: Contentment.

I had heard about this country and long ago decided it was a dangerous place, one to be avoided. Wasn't it bland, boring, and mind-numbing there? Didn't it seduce you into forgetting your responsibility to solve the world's

problems? Wouldn't I lose my passion, my intensity, and my identity as a heroic fighter who is *trying* to beat unbeatable odds? Besides, my ancestors came from the country of Struggle, and who was I to leave my heritage and take up residence in the alien lands of Peace and Plenty?

Being content is a tough, aesthetic choice I am making in my life. If there were a painting of the psychological landscape of my childhood amid alcoholism and of my young-adult years, it would look like a masterpiece sprung from the brush of the American painter Jackson Pollock. Chaos swirls amid intensity of color and movement . . . murky hints of evil and destruction . . . shock and struggle screeching rebelliously from the canvas: "Life!!! Freedom!!!" Whew. Pretty interesting, but hard to live there for long.

I turn to the painting of the landscape that seems to be beckoning to me now. It looks like it's painted by Paul Cezanne. Quiet hills and trees have small homes nestled cozily among them in perfect balance. Soft tones describe a land watered with calm rivers of meaning and interconnection with others. It is not without interest—look! Suddenly a large swan flaps upward to the sky from the inlet where it was just hidden. Can I choose this peaceful valley of contentment? Not yet. I need to understand more about contentment before I do.

One thing I have needed to face up to recently is that experiencing contentment in a situation has nothing to do with the *con*tent of the situation. Contentment is an attitude, a choice of where I will focus my attention. A situation can change completely, and you can remain just as unhappy if you have an attitude of discontent. I learned this by going on vacation. Most of the summer I tend to chafe and moan about living in the middle of a big hot city block. Garbage and broken glass litter the street, and at any time of day or night there is a cacophony of barking dogs, honking horns, drunken fights, and swearing children. This offends my innate preference for beauty and quiet. My family is not in a position to move somewhere else, and it is very easy to get mad and miserable about living here.

This summer I thought I would be able to bear it if we went to the quiet woods for two weeks. I arranged a cabin-on-a-lake-at-a-small-family-resort vacation and comforted myself all summer by glancing at the last two weeks of August outlined in marker on the kitchen calendar. At last the great day came, and we launched out on the escape.

Well, it was quiet. But the cabin was dark, smelly, and claustrophobic. There were tacky pictures on all the walls. The tap water was golden brown. It rained for two days and then remained cloudy and muggy for a few more. There were flies and mosquitoes in the air and a terrifying rumor of leeches in the lake. During the long indoor days my daughter repetitively played her Sesame Street tape or my husband repetitively played Indian raga music. I began to thrash and writhe in discontent! I became a toxic pollutant in our small cabin environment, and my husband and daughter sought refuge in games of solitaire and visiting with other families. After several days of this I decided to salvage the remnants of my self-respect and discipline myself into a better attitude. It wasn't easy, but the other choice appeared to be another week of misery and my increasing unpopularity with my family.

In order to achieve a better attitude, I sat down with a notebook and made a list of things I would have preferred about this vacation environment (sweet clean water . . . airy rooms . . . sunny days . . . etc.). I allowed myself to fully savor each preference while telling myself that I would no longer *expect* these things. My expectations and attachments were causing me to suffer. Then I heaved a big sigh and wrote the reasons why being there was a gift and a blessing. I listed everything positive that had occurred there so far, and without trying very hard, my plus list outweighed the minus list two to one. I acknowledged gratitude for these things and shifted my focus of attention for the rest of the week. We had a good time.

I saw once again that every circumstance has a front and a back, and that my contentment lies in my ability to choose the focus of my attention. Some people say that contentment is "wanting what you have." I now see that in any given situation, *some goal of mine is being fulfilled.* I am not a victim of anything! I may not perceive that I am getting what I need because I have both short-term and long-term goals in operation. There are times when some of them are on hold while others are getting their due. I think that the art of contentment lies in the ability to see how I am reaping what I have asked for.

Four years ago I earnestly asked God to give me complete and unshakable self-esteem. I heard an inner voice say, "Fine. You've got it. It will take you five years to attain that." Ever since then I have been in situations that are directly nurturing my self-esteem or challenging it to the roots. In the more difficult scenarios, I choose to see that this is an answer to my prayer and an opportunity to gain on my goal.

In the case of my stressful urban environment, I am not meeting my short-term goal of getting a good night's sleep. But I am meeting my short-term goal of living cheaply so I don't have to work long hours. I have lots of family and leisure time that I wouldn't have if I were struggling to make a large mortgage payment. I am also being forced to work on some important long-term spiritual goals: cultivating *inner* peace and developing enough humility to see God in all persons. If I choose, I can see this city block as the best learning laboratory to achieve these golden goals.

The process of living in contentment is threefold.

First, the experience of healthy discontent arises because we have some practical or spiritual needs that must be met.

Second, we create short- or long-term goals to meet those needs and observe contentedly the manner in which the goals are being realized.

And third, we need to be realistic about the impermanence and unpredictability of life and willing to let go of each and every one of these desires or attainments when it is time.

I was once crying bitterly to God about how betrayed I felt because all the people I love could be taken away from me. I have no ultimate control. I heard that inner voice say, "I haven't let you down. I never told you that you could keep anybody. It's not part of the deal here."

Everything is impermanent. Jobs, homes, people, your body. It is as if each of these things were a mere container that would only hold what you filled it with—love or fear. The containers are continuously invented and maintained for a while. Then they either gently deteriorate or abruptly break apart. Imagine! What if you approached your whole life with the delight and detachment with which you sit in the sun and blow soap bubbles from a toy wand! When you set out to blow bubbles you fully expect them to be impermanent, yet you do it anyway. You want to see how many you can make at once, how big they can be, how long they can last, and in what manner they will eventually break. You treasure each unique rainbow-streaked sphere for as long as it lasts, confident that there will always be more for as long as you choose to play.

This is my painting of contentment. I will not choose the painting of the quiet valley by Cezanne. There could always be bulldozers in the future. I will choose a painting that shows a sweet-faced person sitting on a mountain blowing bubbles into the air. The person seems innocent, comfortably vulnerable to life. Perhaps it takes a certain amount of deliberate innocence to live a life of contentment these days. And the lofty perch on the mountain gives the person just the right perspective on things. Face-to-face with the

Creator, this person blows beautiful, delicate creations that grace the world for a while and then pass on their way—as the Creator does with each one of us.

Don't worry!—
whatever is supposed to happen will happen—
it never fails!
Face everything contentedly
while absorbing your mind in God.
—*Lalleshwari*

Intuition

"*I* don't know. It's just a gut-level feeling." "It's just a hunch." "It's women's intuition." It's funny how deprecating we sound about that quiet knowing that comes right out of our souls. That's what intuition is—the prompting of our souls to go toward the paths that will bring us the highest good in our lives. It speaks to us in different ways. To some people it is the "still small voice" within. To others, it comes as a picture in the mind in either the waking state or the dream state. It can be a gut-level feeling, a sense of emotional comfort or discomfort. Or it can be a flash of full-blown *knowing* that drops suddenly into our consciousness from out of the blue, bringing information or inspiration.

Most of us repress the strength of intuition and insist that it be subordinate to the logical mind. We regard intuition as an unsettling, possibly embarrassing, second cousin to the functions of logic, control, and linear thinking that we have been trained to rely on. We ignore our intuition's polite suggestions for so long that it either atrophies into total silence or it finds loud, dramatic ways of getting through to us. Sometimes we don't listen to what we know until life pulls us off the road in some crisis that forces us to give up our reliance on the logical "shoulds" in our minds.

Your intuition is trying to show you only one thing all of the time: how to be happy as you. It's there to make life easier. Your intuition will help you understand and unfold your purpose here, and solve everyday problems. It needs to be reinstated on the throne next to the logical mind, where the two can work as partners. Your intuition receives vision for a life-direction that will make you happy and will use your unique nature to the fullest. Your planning mind makes a strategy. But it can't make an airtight strategy because there are always unknowns. Your intuition works through these unknowns, bringing ideas and resources into play right in the present moment.

Your logical mind organizes information; it balances your checkbook. Your intuition balances your life. It tells you about health needs, connects you with good friends, and helps you with timing. It leads you into situations that elicit joy. Together, the intuition and the logical mind create a fulfilling and effective life.

Intuition operates in large and small ways. A number of years ago my intuition showed me in a dream that I needed to relocate to a different city as soon as possible. My logical mind was appalled and embarrassed—I had no reason to go there, and I had school to finish in my hometown. I had a lot of friends and family who would be sad and mystified at my move. But it was a strong feeling, so I did it. I met my beloved husband in a grocery store on my first venture into town. We fell in love instantly. And my health improved dramatically. I had been sick with a variety of complaints for almost two years. Now I discovered that I had been a creature at odds with my old environment, and I could be more relaxed and healthy in my new location.

My intuition helps me with smaller challenges too. While I was driving around on errands my little voice said, *Go home right now.* My logical mind told me I needed to go to the store first. *Really, right now. Go home.* My logical mind whined as I turned toward home, prematurely, as far as it was concerned. As I entered my front door, the phone was ringing. It was a person I had tried to get in touch with unsuccessfully for two weeks. We made a quick little transaction that eased my current work project, and I went back out, smiling.

How to Strengthen Intuition

Acknowledge that it's there. Even if it has atrophied from disuse, your intuition can be awakened and brought back into your life. Talk to it. Say, "I know you're there. I'd like you to be working in my life. Please become active for my highest good."

Notice how your intuition speaks to you. Do you hear a little voice, almost like the rest of your thoughts but not quite? Do you see pictures in your mind? Do you *know* things but doubt that you know them because you don't have actual proof? Does your body give you cues about whether certain people are trustworthy? Discover which of these modes is strongest and focus on that one.

Take some risks. Start small, but start following those little hunches instead of your conditioned brain. See where your own energy *wants* to go, not where you think it *should* go. Do something because it feels right, not because it makes sense. Follow the spiritual impulse.

Trial and error. Good discrimination between the intuitive mind and the conditioned mind takes time and practice. Don't doubt everything just because you're wrong sometimes. *Decide* to be accurate with intuition and keep practicing.

Become willing to flow more in your life. Let your life be easier. Cultivate an appetite for synchronicity and surprise. Being in control all of the time is exhausting and unimaginative. Let the creativity of the Universe into your life and enjoy!

> *(now the ears of my ears awake and*
> *now the eyes of my eyes are opened)*
> —*e. e. cummings*

Humility

Blessed are the meek, for they shall inherit the earth.
—Matthew 5:5

*T*en years ago when I started therapy, my counselor observed that I seemed to be a person with a great deal of power and energy that I was scattering to the winds with my erratic, undisciplined behavior. She asked me why I was afraid to have power. I replied that I had been taught by my religious upbringing that I should be humble and not call attention to myself or ask for too much for myself. She looked at me and asked, "But what does humility really mean to *you?*" To my surprise, my voice answered from an inner knowing: "Humility is taking one's rightful place in the Universe." My attempt to understand and live this inner truth has been a fascinating process ever since.

Humility has really gotten a bad rap. Generally, people think of humility as taking the "lowest" position in a situation. I have found that there are no real "high" or "low" positions in the world—there is only the right place for each individual at a given time and place within the organic Whole. Some have rejected the idea of adopting humility as an attitude because they were erroneously trained in shame and self-deprecation in the name of humility. These people usually shift to a rebellious form of rigid pride and an inflated sense of self as a defense against the pain of this false understanding. I have seen other people choose permanent identification with the poor in the name of humility. Some of these folks feel righteous in their sense of separation from the rich and powerful, yet they may actually be practicing as great a form of arrogance as the people they presume are snobs! Humility is neither high nor low, rich nor poor. It is taking your rightful place *now* and serving the good of the Whole from that place.

I remember a friend of Martin Luther King, Jr., once describing the constant struggle King felt about being in his position in the civil rights movement. He often felt that he was inadequate for the job, that he lacked some of the skills and qualities he perceived were necessary for this leadership. And yet this "place" was continually offered to him by the mysterious force of this powerful movement, and it was his place alone. How fortunate for our whole nation that he had the humility to continue to accept this position despite his nagging insecurity.

Every one of us is gifted in some regard. It seems that our life situations will consistently ask us to serve the good of the Whole with these gifts, which come out of our character and our nature. Our gifts contribute to the balance and health of our human society. I know someone who has an uncanny knack for enhancing the physical comfort of any environment he is in for more than a day. He serves the comfort of those around him with apparent grace and ease; it comes out of who he is. I know someone else who has an intuitive radar for errors and missing details, and he has been an invaluable worker in his jobs in warehouses and mail-order businesses, where these skills really count. Some people are natural counselors, and their good listening skills and easy empathy will attract the upset or needy person at any party or bus stop! Sometimes we find ourselves asking, "Why am I always the one who . . . ?" Well, because you are. So you're the one who volunteered to stay and clean up after the potluck? Good! Do it. Humility asks you to give what you have to give, within practical limits.

I have known some bright and talented people who kept their light under a bushel because they were afraid to shine. They doubted their own motives, their right to take up space; they served a false notion of humility. Every time God offered them an opportunity to shine, they backed off or sabotaged their own efforts so they wouldn't make too big an impact on anything.

If Life is asking you to shine, it is a form of arrogance to refuse it. It is also a lack of perspective. You are not the best or the worst that has ever come along; you are just uniquely you, and it's your turn under the sun to grow and blossom, spread your seeds, and die. What if the prairie flowers refused to bloom because they were afraid that they wouldn't be the best thing on the prairie or that no one would really appreciate their effort? Humility is taking one's rightful place in the Universe.

I was introduced to another definition of humility by Dr. Edith Stauffer, author of *Unconditional Love and Forgiveness*. She teaches that humility is an attitude of perceiving another's needs as he or she sees them and having the desire to serve those needs, if doing so is practical. That'll keep you busy on your spiritual path for a while. Another's needs, as *that person* understands them . . . It is so much easier to think that we know what other people need, what their priorities should be. Other people may be telling us very clearly what they need, in words or behavior, but if we don't have an attitude of humility in operation, we can miss it entirely. We're busy trying to help them with needs we think they "should" have, and we're getting all lathered up about how ungrateful they are for our efforts!

Sometimes the practice of humility takes the form of accepting criticism. I used to have a tendency to feel crushed or very defensive if there was a hint of criticism coming in my direction. Yet many of the real turning points in my development so far have been triggered by facing some uncomfortable truth about myself that someone managed to get through to me. Someone once said, "Your faults are your obstacles, so you should be grateful to others for pointing them out to you."

At this point you may be saying to yourself, "Come on, what are you trying to do, be a *saint?*" Well, yes, I *do* want to be a saint. I have had the privilege of meeting a few souls in this world who have mastered being human—who are saintly— and I have watched them in action. It looks pretty good to me. I have observed that these people are first and foremost *themselves,* their personalities fully open and exalted like a summer rose. I once took a heartfelt problem of mine to such a person, who was surrounded by hundreds of people at the time. But she acted as if there were no one else there. Nothing was more important to her in that moment than serving my need as I understood it. This moment of total, loving attention was like a healing balm for me.

It was in the company of a few souls on Earth that I realized humility is a power as radiant as the sun or as strong as a thundering waterfall in its ability to transform others. Its power is an unimpeded expression of Spirit. I must regard my own efforts at humility with the same tenderness I would a baby bird learning to fly. My relationship to a saint is like that of a baby bird to a grown bird. I must forgive my awkward flapping and falling, and I must smile at the screeches I emit. I trust that one day I will fly in the clear sky of my liberated Spirit.

> *When you are content to be simply yourself*
> *and don't compare and compete,*
> *everybody will respect you.*
> —*Tao Te Ching*

Loss

Loss is something we think of as an exception to normal life, an aberration—except this must be wrong because it happens so often. I have had many losses: a child, a best friend, a family business. If this sort of thing isn't happening to *me* right now, it's happening to someone I know or someone on the news. No matter how much I say that life is unpredictable and beyond my control, it is still a major shock to me every time this proves to be true.

Every time I face a loss I remember a few things. I remember that the Universe is simultaneously dispassionate and compassionate toward its members. It is dispassionate in that it is no respecter of persons; it does not *care* how much money you lost, how embarrassing this scandal is,

how gross the accident was, or how young the children are when a spouse contracts a terrible illness. This cool dispassion is the meaning behind the esoteric slogan, "S _ _ _ happens."

On the other hand, the Presence within this Universe is at the same time completely compassionate toward us when we are suffering through anything, large or small. When I am reeling from sudden loss, I turn vulnerably toward that Presence, and I find myself in a warm pocket of peace and benevolence amid my grief. My heart opens in love and compassion for myself and others, and I soften into the richness of the present moment. Every need I have is met as fast as I can think of it. Friends and strangers alike become emissaries of this love. At these times I think, *Ah, I understand now. I will remember this.* This is the experience expressed in the new bumper sticker, "Love happens."

Then there is the problem of integrating my loss into daily life. This is difficult to accomplish gracefully. After I have granted myself a certain amount of time to be emotional and get some support, I rally and get back into normal life with thoughts such as *Come on, get back on the ball, back in the saddle, back into production.* But it's hard to accept being with loss for as long as it actually takes to heal from it. I become painfully aware that no one is paying me for all the hours I need to stare into space after a loss. I find myself resisting being soft and vulnerable to the Presence in the way that I was in the midst of the crisis. And there are times when I cannot bear to walk forward for very long with the awareness of my real helplessness.

Yesterday morning I looked out my window and found a hurt sparrow lying on its back out in the cold. I ran outside and scooped it gently into my hands. My intention was to move it to a quiet place away from my dog so it could die undisturbed—its neck was obviously broken. But as I carried it, the bird looked into my eyes with a peaceful curiosity, apparently unafraid. It was still so alive! I didn't have the heart to put someone who was really looking at me down on the hard ground to die.

So I brought him inside. As a child would, I put him in a shoe box with flannel rags and got him some water, which I fed him with an eyedropper. The adult, dispassionate part of me observed my futile behavior with wry acceptance. I knew the bird was going to die. But somehow I had to do this anyway.

My young daughter immediately became absorbed. Even though I warned her that we would try this only for a little while, that the bird would probably die, she became passionately bonded with the bird within moments. She fed him water on the half hour, cooed encouragement, and brought him pictures to look at while he was resting. She kept seeing signs that he was dramatically improving as a result of her faith and effort. I tried to reflect reality to her from time to time, but it was obvious that she couldn't accept it.

The sparrow died that evening. My daughter was stunned and hurt to find the bird still, his bright eyes closed. She threw herself into my arms and cried hot tears while still shaking her head in disbelief. She had to tell me the exact details of her latest nursing efforts, and exactly how he looked when she found him dead. She gazed deeply into space, absorbed in sorrow as we rocked together in the dim room.

This morning, she needed to take his body out

and look at it. Again, the look of grave sorrow on her face. She shook her head a little and sighed, still not quite believing. She insisted that we take several photos of him before putting him back into his burial bag. Then we drew pictures for her to take to school—one of her feeding the living bird with an eyedropper, and one of her crying as she looked at him in death. She showed the pictures to her classmates and told them the story. Tonight, I asked her how she felt about it and she said, "I'm still sad, but not as much. It's passing."

It seems to me that most of us are like children, bonding passionately to people and things with the cry of "Mine!" Then we experience desolation when we discover that they aren't. At these times the Wise One within whispers, "I know this really hurts. This is just the way it is." We rock together in the dim light, pondering, staring into space. And healing comes.

> *I will not forget you. I have carved*
> *you on the palm of my hand.*
> *—Isaiah 49:15*

Getting Up Again

Shakespeare wrote, "All the world's a stage, and all the men and women merely players."

There are times in your life when you feel like an actor in a play that has suddenly been rewritten without warning. There you are, performing your role as you have studied and rehearsed it, and suddenly there is a flurry of stagehands removing the familiar props, and your leading partner is cut from the scene. You stare into dim spaces outside of the footlights, seeking the face of the director, and feebly call, "Line?" Death, injury, divorce, disease, business failure. . . . Who doesn't know the feeling of having the rug pulled out from under you and hitting the hard ground of reality with a thud? We all go through these things at times, and we face the difficult task of getting up again.

The phoenix is an ancient symbol of rebirth, a triumph of the spirit's renewal after apparent destruction. Originating in Egyptian mythology, the phoenix is a bird that consumed itself by fire after five hundred years and rose renewed from its own ashes. It would be nice if people could rise immediately from their wreckage with a flurry of wings and golden sparks flying, but the process is usually more gritty and mundane than that. It looks more like hobbling to your knees, pulling yourself up with some outside support, and leaning on something while you attempt to breathe evenly. Then you limp slowly forward on a dimly lit trail, the horizon obscured by undergrowth. Eventually your strength returns and your trail meets a larger path and a clear view. Until then you have to proceed with an ample supply of support, perspective, hope, and will.

When you are suffering from a personal loss or catastrophe, it helps to get some support from others who really understand your situation. You are not alone. There are others who are going through something like this right now, and they may have a larger compassion and bigger ears for the details of your sorrow than your friends who are tired of hearing about it. These days, there are support groups for just about everything you can think of.

There are also experts who can offer some experienced perspectives on your recovery process. It helps to hear that you are dealing with something that many others have faced, that it was not a personal attack on you for some imagined unworthiness. We need to be reminded that healing takes time. I have heard that it takes at least three years to grieve and integrate the divorce of a long marriage. When my friend fell off a roof and was paralyzed from the neck down, a rehabilitation therapist told him that it takes an average of five years to come to acceptance and happiness after such a change.

Recently I realized that hope is not a *feeling*, it is a *discipline*. Hope is a set of behaviors and attitudes you adopt to carry you forward as if your life matters, even though at the moment you may feel that it doesn't. When you are facing a time of heavy emotion and lack of direction, it is an act of hope to tend to health habits like eating and sleeping and to keep a minimum level of beauty and order in your appearance and environment. When sailors are kept ashore by stormy seas, they mend nets and clean the boat for future sailing because they know that the storm is finite and work at sea will call them again.

It is natural to experience depression after a major loss. It is the discipline of hope that prevents the depression from getting too great a hold on you and settling in for a long time. Vitamins, exercise, fresh air, and sunlight will help your body continue to clear through this stress. Listening to music, especially stringed instruments, is a balm for a sore heart and jangled nerves. A good hearty cry in someone's arms is certainly called for too. You can discipline yourself to stop negative self-talk in your mind and switch your thoughts to positive statements instead. And though you may feel lacking in spiritual inspiration at the moment, you can build your physical strength and will until vision is kindled in your life again.

Your will is the spiritual mechanism by which goals are attained and new dreams manifested. If you are experiencing a lack of dreams or goals, you can still go about the business of strengthening and toning your will until it has a new job to do. Establishing a routine and sticking to it is one way of strengthening your will. Rhythmic exercise, listening to drumming music, and accomplishing small distasteful tasks will also help. I strengthen my will by insisting that I be punctual for appointments—I am usually ten minutes late. Strengthening the will is done by the same principles as strengthening muscles on an exercise machine: isolate and focus on a number of small individual tasks in your life and work on each of them regularly. It may seem silly or futile some days, but strength of will builds, and eventually a zest for a new challenge does too. And when that zest is there, it attracts inspiration for new roles and goals in your life. At this point you can usually look back at your earlier catastrophe and feel some appreciation for its occurrence, and sometimes you can even see how it was necessary for this previous attachment to be wrestled out of your hands.

History provides us with numerous examples of people getting up after having the wind knocked out of them. Wars and earthquakes have ripped their way through the human race time after time, leaving wounds and wreckage in their wake. And yet cities get rebuilt and people fall in love again. Poets sing the stories of heroes, and mothers cry their impassioned "Why?" to caring witnesses. The experience of loss and getting up again is an integral part of the human adventure.

I learned something special about the spaceship sent as an ambassador to unknown civilizations outside our solar system. Among the various artifacts of human culture is a piece of music chosen to represent the human spirit. Out of ten thousand songs that were proposed, the song that speeds toward our unknown fellows in the universe is a Bulgarian folk song that is a message of mourning, strength, determination, and the thirst for freedom. It is wonderful that our scientists chose to be vulnerable to the unknown witnesses out in the universe, to say in effect, "Hi! We're here. It isn't easy. But we keep getting up again."

> *After the final no there comes a yes*
> *and on that yes the future of the world depends.*
> —*Wallace Stevens*

Transformation

I've always believed in the possibility that a major planetary transformation for the better will occur in the course of my lifetime. That belief is being sorely tested in this time of world-wide chaos. It appears to me as if the quality of human consciousness is at an all-time low, with ignorance, denial, and addiction still reigning in my world. I am tempted to draw some negative conclusions about the results of all this, except for three things: (1) The winds of truth are blowing strongly in my life and the lives of everyone I know, (2) I feel my own consciousness traveling to a new level, and (3) My hopeless city block is undergoing a mysterious transformation. And believe me, if this block can do it, so can the rest of the planet!

After the Gulf War "ended" and most of the nation settled in to enjoy the "win" like the afterglow of the Superbowl, I turned the television off. I haven't watched it since. Something became hard and clear and focused inside me, and I entered a vigorous campaign to know and speak and live the truth in my personal life. Oddly enough, it seems as though most of my friends became involved in a similar program at the same time. One of my friends refers to the program as "Promoting Reality." She has decided to calmly "promote reality" in all of the daily situations she's in, no matter how thick the isolation or denial in the people around her. I wonder if the winds of truth blowing around here are circulating their effects to other parts of the world. Wouldn't it be great if our world leaders and our media would choose "Promote Reality" as their slogan?

Meanwhile, something's happening to me too. After meditating regularly for years, my meditation is now noticeably different. My mind is settling into silence almost effortlessly. I am able to spend time with people I formerly detested and enjoy an attitude of love and respect for them, even though they haven't changed a bit! I am able to work with people in my new mode of calm, head-on truth, and we are all flowering. I am getting more serious about my complete personal liberation, and God is meeting me with the same degree of earnestness.

One night I dropped to my knees and prayed to be released from my stressful approach to daily life. That night I had a dream in which I saw my mind as if it were a house. It was a house of torture! Each of the rooms represented a self-defeating thought or fear, all interconnected in a structure designed to give me no rest or peace. I woke up and realized that fundamentally, I need to acknowledge that I *deserve* to experience peace of mind and that I do not need to torture myself. Now, every few nights, I have a long dream that explores one of these rooms in my mind, and I work through many aspects of it. Then I wake up in a state of new quiet and understanding. My prayer is being answered, and I feel more trust because I see I am in expert hands!

I recognize the same talent at work on my city block. It is a mystery to me why I live here, except that I love my house and it's the place for me to be now. I'd rather live in a quiet-aesthetic-prosperous-eco-village-on-beautiful-land-with-serene-responsible-people place. Instead, I moved to a block that contains an energy vortex of crime, chaos, and generalized ugliness. The blocks nearby us are fine—it's just *this* one that seems like a hot spot in our neighborhood.

When we moved in, we soon learned that the two houses to the south of us were owned by people who sponsored parties and fights on a regular basis. In the fourplex across the street the tenants left piles of trash and stolen grocery carts in front of the building. The house on the other side of us was occupied by a single mother with seven kids who was too tired and overwhelmed to enforce curfew or civil behavior. Then there was the crack house down the block with cars pulling up and honking at all hours.

After a number of sleepless nights that first summer, I bottomed out somewhere in mid-July. I cried and raged at God about my miserable fate and swore hatred and revenge upon my ignorant neighbors. In the middle of my hysteria, my Higher Self whispered to me that I was in a lesson about taking a stand. I come from an alcoholic family, and as a child I learned to adapt to inappropriate behavior passively rather than confront it intelligently. Now it was clear that I needed to take a stand about the quality of my environment. Nothing less than transformation would do.

I approached this challenge on several levels. On a practical level, I put energy into beautifying my property and picking up garbage whenever it appeared. I calmly and firmly informed my neighbors *every time* their noise kept me awake at night. On a political level, I got acquainted with my neighborhood organizations, alderman, and Community Crime Prevention. I wrote letters to landlords; I called the police. On a spiritual level, I prayed for the lady next door, the slumlord across the street, and for the block in general. I forgave everyone for our lifestyle differences and prayed that everyone would find his or her rightful place.

Once a week I went up and down the block with a bag, picking up garbage. This was both a practical and a spiritual exercise. I felt conspicuous and foolish, angry that I was taking responsibility for the mess others had created. So I breathed deeply and thought about Mother Teresa picking up diseased bodies in Calcutta. She sees God in every one of those people. I quietly chanted prayers while I worked and pretended to see God in everything too. I practiced a mind-set of loving neutrality as I picked up sticky junk-food wrappers, cigarette butts, and cans dripping beer. I breathed away judgment of the people who left them there.

After about a month of this, the garbage appeared less and less. The block began to stay clean for weeks at a time. Over the next six months, a number of changes occurred. The woman next door became friends with an energetic young man who had a lot of time and talent to help nurture and discipline her kids. The invisible slumlord sold his building to a responsible, accessible man who gave it a face-lift.

The people on the other side of me decided to sell, and a sweet, gentle woman who loves to garden moved in. The crack house down the street went into foreclosure and is being purchased by a man who is committed to the neighborhood. The city is planning on removing some of the most run-down houses to cut down on urban density. The change in the atmosphere on this block is palpable, and a number of neighbors have been commenting on it. "Getting better," they say.

I'm not really the one who is *doing* all of these things around here. But I am seeing that all it takes is a committed minority to accelerate the rate of positive evolution in any given situation. The world situation is teetering so evenly between getting better and getting worse that more of us need to add our weight to the constructive momentum. Come on, friends! Join the movement to promote reality! The place to change the world is *here,* in *your* life, and the time is *now.* Add a little truth, a little grit, some politics, and some prayer. Focus it with your will and deliver it with love. And we shall overcome.

Will transformation. Oh be inspired
*   for the flame*
in which a Thing disappears and bursts
*   into something else;*
the spirit of re-creation which masters
*   this earthly form*
loves most the pivoting point where
*   you are no longer yourself.*

— *Rainer Maria Rilke*

111

Spiritual Commitment

I have been living in a gale wind of growth for a long time. I feel like a beautifully faceted cluster of amethyst that is partially covered with clumps of sand and grit. Some craftsperson in the employment of the Divine is holding me carefully in his hand and blasting away at the grit covering my beauty with a high-pressure air tool. The grit consists of the fear, rigidity, and willfulness that obscures my radiance and the true shapes and contours of who I am. Some of it flies off easily. Some of it is very stubborn and requires repetitive applications of gentle solvent to gradually work it loose. I am afraid. I am afraid to sparkle unafraid. But I know that I will because I am committed.

That's the trouble when you give yourself wholeheartedly to the evolution of your higher consciousness—eventually it works! I have been on a vigorous spiritual journey for many years. I have marched out of the clutches of addiction and codependency. I left struggle behind a few miles back. The road is curving into lands of self-esteem and shining personal success. As I look up the road ahead I have the eerie sensation that the picture is turning from black and white into full color. Where's the fear? I'm afraid because I see no fear there! I want to sit down on the road where it still looks familiar and cuddle up to an addictive substance or two.

When I was a child I stopped my playing in awe one day to see a black man on television speaking to a lot of people. His radiant face and awesome oration spoke of his dream for a world without hate or suffering. My hair stood up all over my body and rivers of tingles bathed me as tears streamed steadily down my face. I realized that this man was working in service of the truth. I wanted to do that too. I understood then that the only thing that really mattered to me was to grow up to be wise and free and to help other people do so too. I am a spiritual worker. Now my prayer is to accept the real possibility that I will reap the fruits of my labor. The time for it is at hand.

I have given myself to the cause of the evolution of human consciousness. I work on my own consciousness by being obedient to the healing directions coming from my Higher Self, and as I master a facet of it, people begin to come to me for help with the very same thing. There are people ahead of me on the continuum of consciousness. They guide and inspire me to greater self-mastery, as I hope to guide and inspire others. It's not a hierarchy of being better than another person. It's more like the color spectrum of white light seen through a prism—a continuum of consciousness vibrating in different colors, yet all parts of one Being.

I want you to give yourself wholeheartedly to the evolution of human consciousness too. Starting in your own life, today, make an athletic leap to the higher ground that you know is calling you. There is no more room, no more time for fear or withholding from truth and love in our world. Come out of fear and control and submit to living your love and inner beauty in your daily engagements. All the help you could possibly need is right here, now. Agree to shine in service of truth. Become committed.

A better world will not arise out of the manipulation of existing political and economic forms. It will happen out of a shift in our consciousness as a whole. The relationship of form to consciousness is like the relationship of plants to soil. If you significantly alter the pH balance in the soil, old plants will die out and different ones will thrive. We are changing the pH balance of humanity's consciousness by composting our fears and planting seeds of love and selfless service. A new world is coming in a mysterious manner that we can barely predict and cannot control. It may take many more years for this shift to be complete, but it's coming. All we can do is submit joyfully to our uncomfortable role as evolutionary mutations of our species.

I know of a fine spiritual teacher whose journey took him from a small village to a meditation path in the Himalayas. He was then led to do political work in India. He worked long and hard with the best minds and resources available to address the problems of hunger and poverty there.

He concluded at last that these efforts would be ultimately ineffective until there was a large-scale change in human consciousness. He now teaches meditation and the *Course in Miracles* to twenty serious students, who then teach it to others. Occasionally he goes into periods of retreat for extended meditation. He is a spiritual worker.

Mother Teresa is one of the most respected people of our time. This is noteworthy, because what she is doing doesn't look successful in terms of our popular culture's glamour-and-profit mind-set. She and her sisters give their complete attention to the poorest of the poor at the hour of their death. Why do we respect that so much? Because we unconsciously recognize that she is serving the evolution of consciousness, which we are part of. If one lost person on the other side of the earth regains his memory of love and his own worth for two minutes in his whole life just before he dies, something great has been accomplished for all of us. Mother Teresa is a spiritual worker.

Several years ago three spiritual masters from different meditation traditions left their home-lands to teach meditation on a large scale to seek-ers around the world. One of them, Baba

Muktananda of India, said that the voice of his guru commanded him to do this and be part of a revolution of consciousness. When asked why this was happening now, he replied simply, "Sometimes such a time comes." He was a spiritual worker.

This is not to say that meditation is the answer for everybody—it is not wise to jump superficially into a meditation practice. It requires commitment and is best undertaken after a certain amount of physical and emotional housecleaning takes place. The higher ground is different for everyone along the continuum. Maybe you can volunteer in a World Peace run or walk for AIDS or be a Big Brother or Big Sister. Maybe you need to grow in recovery or improve your diet or get into therapy or make a commitment with another person to be honest with each other. Every bit of your self-effort helps every one of us too.

Our world today is like a lovely old house that is in serious disrepair because it has been destroyed by tenants living in ignorance and disrespect of themselves and others. There is garbage everywhere, broken windows, and holes punched in walls. On the continuum of consciousness, people in recovery are like individuals who have stopped participating in the destruction and are getting their bearings. Spiritual workers are like a sturdy work crew descending on the house on a long Saturday to clean and repair the damage and restore it to its original glory with some thoughtful modern improvements. Is this worth it? Will this really make a difference? Yes. Let's have some reinforcements and keep going. Will you be committed too?

> *There are no passengers on Spaceship Earth.*
> *Everybody's crew.*
> —*Marshall McLuhan*

More titles for the spiritual searcher . . .

Trusting Intuition

by Helene Lerner-Robbins

Trust yourself. You can have faith in your personal and spiritual progress. These innovative meditation books bolster your self-confidence and affirm that you are where you need to be in your journey of self-discovery. 96 pp.

My Timing Is Always Right

There are no coincidences and no mistakes. You are in the right place. Overcome worry and anxiety about the frustrations of daily situations. Discover why people, places, and things are as they should be—right now—in your life. 96 pp.

Order No. 5471

Embrace Change

When old ways no longer work and new behaviors still feel uncomfortable, *Embrace Change*. These affirmations and meditations help you make the most of the day and focus on continuing personal growth. Find renewed courage for making changes in your attitudes, ideas, projects, and relationships. 96 pp.

Order No. 5470

Green Spirituality

Reflections on Belonging to a World Beyond Myself

by Veronica Ray

When you wonder, "What am I becoming spiritual for?" read *Green Spirituality*. Veronica Ray's meditations place special emphasis on moving beyond personal growth. This beautiful book is about caring for the human community—considering "Myself and Others," "Myself and Community," and "Myself and the Earth." 128 pp.

Order No. 5184

HAZELDEN EDUCATIONAL MATERIALS

800-328-9000   **612-257-4010**   **612-257-1331**

(Toll Free. U.S.,   (Outside the U.S.   (FAX)
Canada & the   & Canada)
Virgin Islands)

Pleasant Valley Road • P.O. Box 176 • Center City, MN 55012-0176

HAZELDEN EUROPE • P.O. Box 616 • Cork, Ireland
Telephone: Int'l Code+353+21+314318
24-Hour FAX: Int'l Code+353+21+961269